becoming y

Green Balloon Publishing

other publications by vivian broughton include:

in the presence of many: reflections on constellations emphasising the individual context

the heart of things: understanding trauma – working with constellations

several articles in professional journals

she has also edited all the english translations of franz ruppert's books

becoming your true self

a handbook for the journey from trauma to healthy autonomy

revised and updated 2017

by vivian broughton

drawings by karen mcmillan

based on the identity-oriented psychotrauma therapy
theories and practice of professor franz ruppert, munich

healing doesn't mean the damage never existed.
it means the damage no longer controls your life.
(unknown author)

Green Balloon Publishing

First published in the United Kingdom in 2014
by Green Balloon Publishing

revised and updated 2014, 2016, 2017

© V. Broughton 2014, 2016, 2017

Green Balloon Publishing
Steyning, UK
www.greenballoonbooks.co.uk
info@greenballoonbooks.co.uk

ISBN 978-0-9559683-5-8

Book production by The Choir Press, Gloucester

Set in Helvetica

preface to revised edition

Identity-oriented Psychotrauma Therapy is the development of Professor Dr Franz Ruppert, professor of psychology and psychotherapist at the University of Applied Sciences in Munich. It is a comprehensive theory of psychological and emotional trauma combined with an effective treatment method. This book aims to provide a brief and friendly introduction to these ideas as a way of bringing this vital topic to a more general attention.

This, third, revised version of this book includes updated information about identity, and the trauma of identity ... the first and primary trauma of our life. This trauma happens in the making of our first relationship, with our mother, if that relationship cannot honour us as a unique individual with our own wants and needs, separate and distinct from the needs and wants of our mother. If we have suffered from a Trauma of Identity this will influence our whole life. Ruppert suggests that from then on our life is a life under the influence of trauma. He calls this our 'traumabiography'.

This book is intended for anyone wishing to explore and heal their own personal trauma. While it is likely to be of interest to professional psychotherapists and counsellors, it is not intended as a study of how to work professionally with trauma, with Professor Ruppert's theories of trauma and attachment, or the Intention Method. This subject matter is covered in my book, *The Heart of Things: Understanding trauma – working with constellations,* and all of Franz Ruppert's books, published in English by Green Balloon Publishing, UK, www.greenballoonbooks.co.uk.

Note on gender terms: I have attempted to vary usage between genders as much as possible. However, since much of the text is discussing the child's relationship with the mother, I have frequently used the male term for the child to help with clarity, so the child is 'he' and the mother 'she'. However everything said of course also applies to female children.

My thanks to Karen McMillan for her lovely drawings to illustrate the text.

Hi!

This book is dedicated to the many people who have been, and continue to be, willing to put their trust in me, and what I do. I have learned more from them than from anyone else, and their lives and stories continually touch mine in ways that they cannot know.

contents

contents

welcome!

It may seem weird to start a book on psychological trauma with a 'welcome' … but I want this book to be welcoming *because* it is about trauma, and because it is also about how to overcome trauma, and become a healthy, autonomous human with a clear sense of identity, capable of establishing healthy and loving relationships.

I believe trauma is the most pervasive and unaddressed issue of our society; it affects all of us, individually, collectively, socially and globally. It profoundly affects our ability to be autonomous and self-responsible, to know who we really are, and our ability to make and maintain constructive and satisfying relationships. It also affects our ability to be parents to our own children.

Because no one can heal anyone else's trauma, we must start with the individual … you, and me, and this book is an invitation to you to think about yourself from a different perspective, the perspective of identity and of trauma.

This invitation will take you on a journey from your conception, through your incubation to birth, early infancy, childhood and thence into adulthood, and we will do this from the perspective of understanding the impact of arriving in a context (your family) that may itself be traumatised, confused and confusing. We will also look at what it means to have a healthy identity, a healthy 'I', to know who you really are and what you really want, and how early traumas undermine this, and then what you can do about it.

If you are here, then you have taken a step, and I welcome you on this journey. I hope that what you read may offer some insight into your experiences, and that you feel

encouraged to take further steps along the way. Coming out of a trauma is a step-by-step process. It can't be rushed, and only you can know what you are ready for in any moment. It is a journey into a true and real relationship with yourself, as the most important person in your life, a journey towards coming to know yourself as you truly are. Trauma tends to foster illusions so as to avoid the reality of the trauma, so truth and 'reality as it is', are the currency of trauma healing.

First, to get two initial problems out of the way:

1. Many of us do not know that we have suffered a trauma.
2. Even if we do know we have suffered a trauma, it is hard for us to know what the real impact of it is and how to deal with it.

This is because our instinctive reaction to a trauma experience is to avoid it and the feelings involved. In fact avoiding the experience of trauma is the way we humans have developed over millennia for surviving traumatic situations. How do we do this? By dissociating ourselves from the experience, thereby splitting it off from our conscious mind, and banishing it to the depths of our unconsciousness.

However making it unconscious and avoiding our trauma means that we remain a hostage to it. From our unconscious the unresolved trauma exercises its influence; then we are not in charge of ourselves or of our life, but instead we may feel increasingly out of control. The paradox of trauma is that the very means of our survival at the time of the trauma, in the aftermath becomes the cause of limitations in our life. It disrupts our ability to be success-ful in our endeavours, to have good relationships, to be happy, confident, effective and clear in our choices and decisions, to feel love and to be loved.

From the ravages of trauma emerges a new self, the 'surviving self', and over time we come to mistake this self for who we actually are. This becomes our 'identity'. Understanding this 'surviving self' as a step towards discovering who we *really* are, and increasing our healthy ability and understanding as to how we can resolve our unconscious trauma is the purpose of this book.

Understanding something gives some sense of authority and mastery. If we understand what trauma is, its impact on us, and how that impact grows and develops, we can feel less intimidated and more able to think and act usefully. However, reading this book alone will not heal your trauma. As of this time I do not believe that we can heal the internal psychological splits that result from trauma on our own, but only in therapy with a practitioner who understands trauma from this perspective. This is exactly *because* our innate reaction to trauma is to avoid it, and the surviving part of our self demands that we do so, and so persistently overrides our healthy desire to heal ourselves.

However there is much that you *can* do to support your journey, and I hope what you find here helps you to do that. If you are working with a therapist who understands trauma in this way, I hope that the contents of this book will be a continuing resource and support on that journey. If you are not working with such a therapist, perhaps this book will give you the confidence and clarity to make the decision to find one.

This is not a book you have to read right through all in one go. That may suit you, but it may not. Trust yourself in your approach to this book, because when it comes down to it you are the only one who knows what is best for you ... and remember, less is more. If you get to a point where you want to do something else, just go ahead. This may be you telling yourself you've had enough, for now.

why bother?

Many of us manage our life quite well and, despite being conscious of some limitations, it seems good enough. Often we believe that the limitations we experience (such as not being able to achieve success as we would like in our work, or not feeling altogether comfortable and at ease in our relationship) are just the way things are; we believe that we are just like that and there's nothing to be done.

Others find that increasingly they are unable to manage their life; things get worse and they find themselves more and more out of control; relationships keep failing, repeating patterns of disappointment and dissatisfaction occur; they never feel happy or at ease, they never quite fulfil their potential in the areas they would like to. These are extremely common experiences that most of us can recognise in ourselves at some point in our lives.

Even further, some find their lives veering seriously out of their control. They may find themselves on an increasingly downward spiral of self-destruction, addictions, self-harm and chaotic and uncontrolled behaviours and experiences, feeling a victim to life rather than the author of their life.

My answer to the question "Why bother?" for the first group is: why not? Why not see if those limitations can respond to exploration and consideration?

And for the second group my answer would be: in a way you have no choice. You have to do something or things are likely to get worse.

And for the third group: my hope is that you will find some explanations in this book that can make sense to you of your confusing experiences, and set you on a positive road to healing.

I believe we can resolve trauma, in fact I am in no doubt about it. But we have to understand what 'resolving trauma' means, and this is best summed up by a quotation I found on the internet by an unknown author:

Healing doesn't mean the damage never existed.

It means the damage no longer controls our lives.

And that is the key: this book is about regaining control of your life, becoming the author of your life, the authority for your life … it's about becoming a healthy, autonomous adult.

but what happens?

Because the experience of the trauma is split off and consigned to the unconscious, like the proverbial 'elephant in the room', it is always there and influences every moment . . . we are a hostage to these unconscious forces. Usually we can't talk about it *because* it is unconscious (and probably because our first trauma is from a very early pre-verbal time of our life), and our natural instinct is to look away and get on with something else. Over time this becomes the habit of our lives, with perhaps an increasing amount of our activity being focused on stepping around the elephant, looking away, distracting ourselves, keeping others, even those we love, at a distance in case they inadvertently put us in touch with the 'elephant'. Thus the unresolved trauma gains control, and we lose command of our life.

The fact of a trauma never disappears. It happened. But through understanding, self-awareness, and working with a good therapy that focuses on integration of the psychological splits that trauma causes, we *can* regain healthy control and authority over our lives.

What have you got to lose? And more importantly, what have you got to gain? My answer to the second question is: yourself.

what is autonomy?

Before we look at trauma, let's first briefly look at the healthy end result we are looking for: healthy autonomy and healthy relational ability.

A healthy person lives her life in the creative tension between two poles:

symbiosis – the ability to be in intimate relationship

and

autonomy – the ability to be self-governing and independent

The word 'symbiosis' means 'living together', and it means being in a mutually beneficial and creative relationship. The word 'autonomy' refers to our individuality, our separateness and our unique identity; our ability to be the author and authority of our life. We are never completely in symbiosis or autonomy. When we are more in autonomy our relational ability is more in the background, and when we are more in intimate relationship, our autonomy may be somewhat in the background.

a healthy person is ...

... able to be in intimate relationship with others (symbiosis), without having to give up on herself, maintaining a sense of a separate self-authorising individual (autonomy). Her opinion of herself comes primarily from herself, and she is not dependent on the good opinion of others for her sense of self. She can make good, clearly thought through choices and decisions, is happy with her own company, and yet does not fear or need to avoid intimate relationships. We could call this having a healthy sense of 'I'.

That is the creative relationship between our symbiotic ability and our autonomous ability.

The effect of trauma is that it seriously injures our identity and our ability to be autonomous, because the trauma situation is one in which we have no choice, we are entirely at the mercy of the situation and our autonomy is denied, even obliterated. This often has a profound impact on our subsequent ability to take charge of our life, to make independent assessments and choices and to have a good sense of self. We become trapped in the unhealthy symbiosis of the victim with the perpetrator.

A person who has suffered trauma tends to ...

- be unhappy, even frightened, when alone
- crave company and companionship . . .
- . . . but also is frightened of relationship and intimacy
- may feel safer, even though unhappy, when alone
- easily feels abandoned
- seeks the approval of others
- finds it hard to make decisions and think clearly
- tends to devolve decision-making and authority to others
- when with others tends to feel 'merged', non-separate and confused
- tends to feel helpless and is easily overwhelmed
- may become authoritarian, arrogant and opinionated as a defence

Many of us will recognise some of these as features of who we are and how we live our life, and we will look further into this later on.

The contention of this book is that the underlying cause of our inability to become healthy autonomous adults is trauma. We know about some of the more obvious traumas of childhood, such as sexual abuse, violence and neglect, and the later traumas that may happen in our teens and youth. But underneath any such traumas lies the issue of early trauma, which may have happened before we have any cognitive memory, maybe even before our birth. These are what we call the 'trauma of identity' and 'the trauma of love', two traumas that result in the deeply disturbing experience of being unwanted and unloved.

These much earlier traumatic experiences are far more difficult to access, understand and admit to, mainly because they occurred in the very earliest time of our life, before conceptual memory and before any kind of cognitive or verbal ability. We can tell the existence of such traumas by the extent to which we are unable to be healthily autonomous.

So for now we will have a look at exactly what constitutes a trauma, how it works, the consequences and how it can affect us.

what is trauma?

a definition

The first step on our journey is to understand exactly what trauma is. We tend to use the word loosely, but if we really want to work with our trauma we need to know precisely what it is. I have four key words that define trauma:

overwhelm

helplessness   =

life-threat

splitting

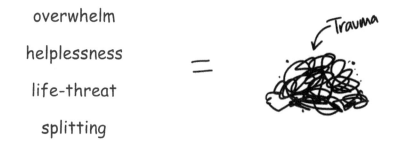

overwhelm – the situation is experienced as completely over-whelming and we lose our capacity for self-regulation of our body and psyche.

helplessness – our experience is of extreme utter helplessness.

life-threat – we fear that we may not survive the situation; we feel our continued existence is threatened; we feel hopeless.

splitting – the psyche splits off the devastating experience as a last ditch survival attempt.

Any event that fulfils all of these criteria in the experience of the victim is a trauma. Yes, I use the word 'victim', because at the time of the trauma situation that is what we were. That is the true meaning of the word 'victim'.

understanding the difference between 'high stress' and 'trauma'

It is important for our purposes of understanding trauma to know the difference between a situation that is a 'high stress' situation and one that constitutes a trauma.

A situation becomes a trauma when our resources for managing stress fail. What do I mean by this? Well, we manage stress by a *hyper-mobilisation* of the body's resources, a highly active state that involves flooding the body with stress hormones, increasing the heart-rate and energy levels in order to support extreme action, most commonly termed 'fight or flight'. This accounts for the extraordinary feats of strength some people are capable of in such situations. The higher the stress, the higher the mobilisation.

The problem is that we can only function at such a highly mobilised state for a short while; the stress on the physiological and psychological systems is very great, and were it to continue, such a hyper-mobilised state would in the end become a danger to our life: quite simply, e.g. our heart would fail. At some point before this the psychosomatic system (the body/mind) flips, quite suddenly, into a *hypo-mobilised* state, an extremely low activity state; this is the point at which we enter the trauma state. So the 'trauma' reaction is in itself a strategy of survival ... Without this flip reaction the high mobilisation in the body itself would kill us.

In the *hyper*-mobilised high stress state the natural reaction is fight *or* flight. We are not completely helpless, we can do something: we can fight or we can flee. The high energy enables us to do one or the other, but we can't do both at the same time, and both need large amounts of energy.

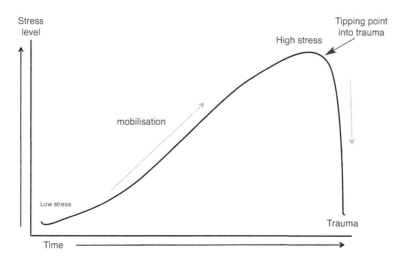

Fig. 1, from high stress to trauma

In the *hypo*-mobilised trauma state we are completely helpless, and the body/psyche gives up, becoming limp. It resigns to its fate. The body's last ditch survival attempt is to withdraw energy and resources back to the centre of the body to try and keep the vital organs going, the heart, lungs, kidneys etc, the parts of ourselves that we cannot live without. This is a situation that is literally about survival, life and death, and everything at this moment focuses on surviving the threat, whatever the cost. The reaction here is known as 'freeze and fragment'. The freezing is the tonic immobility, the 'flop', and the fragmenting is the process whereby the psyche splits off the intolerable experience by disso-ciating from the present reality, relegating it to the unconscious.

the split self after the trauma

The initial means of splitting the experience off is by dissociation: the mind and body disconnects from what is happening and the emotional and psychological experience involved. It is a trance-like state that we can all recognise, an extreme form of 'zoning out'. In our day-to-day life we may dissociate quite often, sometimes in

13

order to focus on something else, as when people are talking but we want to attend to a particular task. That is a healthy and ordered form of dissociation. In the trauma moment the dissociation is automatic, out of our control, protecting us from the intolerable experience of the trauma by sending it to our unconscious. Sometimes the dissociative state is experienced as being separate from the body, outside of oneself, sometimes suspended above oneself.

At this point there emerges a new self, the trauma surviving self. This 'surviving self' is totally preoccupied with avoiding the trauma. The initial characteristic of the surviving self is this dissociative trance-like state, but over the hours, days, weeks and months after the trauma the surviving self gets to work to develop strategies and

structures that guarantee the trauma experience stays out of our awareness. These strategies and structures over time become increasingly sophisticated, subtle and organised, forming many everyday activities and actions that, in the end, we come to think of as who we are, our identity. We mistake this 'self' for our real self.

The split of the psyche becomes increasingly structured and fixed. Here is a diagram representing the split structure of the self after a trauma has happened.

Fig. 2, the split self

14

As you can see, there are three entities to the split, and in order to help you recognise them I will give below some characteristics of each.

Self part	Function	Characteristics
Trauma Self	Holds the trauma memory, experience and feelings	• Is frozen at the time of the trauma • Constantly seeks opportunities to surface into consciousness, to complete itself by expression • Is always at the age of the trauma, so often very young
Trauma Surviving Self	Guards and maintains the boundaries of the splits Develops increasingly complex strategies to do so In later situations of re-traumatisation, if current strategies are insufficient and fail, will develop further splits	• Avoids situations that might re-trigger the trauma • Easily dissociates • Distracts • Seeks to control the environment, others and self • Seeks compensation for lack of joy and pleasant experiences, eg with drugs, alcohol, sex, work • Cannot make good relationships • Does not make clear and good choices & decisions • Lacks clarity • Lacks empathy for self and others • Creates and maintains illusions and delusions such as "everything is fine, there is no problem" or "my childhood was perfectly happy". • Is often confused • Often suffers from inexplicable feelings of shame and guilt
Healthy Self	Yearns for wholeness (integration of splits) Knows something is amiss Tries to heal Seeks help (eg therapy)	• Can think clearly • Seeks truth, honesty and reality • Makes good choices and decisions • Can make good connections and relationships • Is self-responsible and innately ethical and moral • Sexual desires and behaviour are appropriate • Has good memory of past events • Is confident and self-assured • Feelings of guilt and shame are situation appropriate

Fig. 3, characteristics of the split parts

15

After the trauma

- we can still access our healthy self, when we feel safe
- when our trauma is re-triggered, our surviving structures take over
- the traumatised parts of the self are frozen in time, and continually look for opportunity for expression and 'completion' (re-triggering)

more on the trauma surviving self, strategies and structures

While on one level the actions and attitudes of our surviving self have helped us to continue our life, at times its activities and beliefs can leave us feeling perplexed and confused about ourselves. Think of a time when something happened and you acted in a way that, afterwards, you couldn't understand, it was so alien from the person that you like to think you are. You 'lost the plot' before you could think; you lost control of yourself in a tense situation; you reacted in a way that is beyond what you would have liked to have done. These are all indications that your surviving self has been activated because your unresolved trauma was triggered.

Situations that may re-trigger your trauma and so, engage your surviving self:

- any situation where you feel overwhelmed or helpless.
- any situation that may be similar to the original trauma situation (which you may not know).
- any sensory stimulus (smell, sound, image, taste, touch) that may be similar to that of the original trauma situation.
- any situation that involves emotions: the psyche cannot distinguish between the emotions we want to feel and the

unresolved trauma emotions. Once the door is opened to feeling any emotion, such as love, empathy or fear, all the other emotions crowd up together attempting to gain access to consciousness. Thus 'love' can become confused with terror, resulting, for example, in a form of mildly (or not so mildly) suppressed panic or anxiety in intimate situations.

It is important to understand that the trigger for your trauma may be something extremely slight and subtle, something you are not fully conscious of.

All right, so let's look at different types of trauma so that we can understand which types of trauma are likely to affect us in which ways.

different types of trauma

There are two main categories of traumatising situations:

- natural events
- relationship trauma

natural events

These are events such as earthquakes, tsunamis, volcanoes etc. They are the kinds of traumas that we find the easiest to assimilate and recover from. We know that no one is to blame, that these events are part of living on our planet, and we often feel a sense of connection and companionship with others similarly afflicted, and this helps. Traumatisation caused by natural events may be more difficult if we have suffered a prior trauma, because each time we experience a trauma it makes us a bit more vulnerable the next time; a traumatic experience is always in part a re-traumatisation of any previous traumas experienced.

relationship trauma

By this I mean traumas that are to do with our relationship with other human beings. These are more difficult for us to assimilate, and the ease with which we can do this depends on two main criteria:

- *intention:* whether what is perpetrated is perceived as *intentional* (harm is intended) or *accidental* (harm is not intended). Intentional harm usually has a more devastating impact.
- *closeness:* whether the 'perpetrator' is a stranger, or someone we know, such as a friend, work colleague or neighbour, or an intimate bonded person such as a close friend, our partner, mother, father or sibling. The closer the bonded relationship, the more shocking and devastating the effect is likely to be.

categories of traumatisation

Keeping these criteria in mind there are several categories of trauma:

- *trauma of violence:* car accidents or other accidents, war experiences, attacks, rape, attempted murder, muggings, terrorism, torture.
- *sexual trauma:* the trauma of inappropriate, incestuous, abusive, or non-consensual sexual exploitation.
- *early trauma:* this is an existential trauma that happens

pre-birth (in the womb), during birth or in the first phase of existence after birth.

- *trauma of love:* when the infant cannot gain a clear, loving connection with his mother, because the mother cannot or does not love her child.

- *trauma of identity:* the most primary trauma – where the infant has to give up on her healthy identity and healthy wants and identify with her mother's wants and needs – 'identification'.

- *traumatised bonding system:* this is the traumatisation of a whole bonding system, whether a family, workplace, political system or a nation. The process is one that begins with a lack of love and identity (see above). The quest for this failed love becomes a form of persecution as people desperately try to force others to love them. Over the generations the family (or system) becomes increasingly dominated by perpetrator-victim dynamics, based on dominance and submission.

So we will start at the beginning, by looking at our life inside our mother and our birth . . .

beginnings

inside the womb

In the beginning you were two single cells; after fertilisation these cells quickly started to divide and create more and more cells. As you developed in your mother's womb, you were not separate from your mother. You ate what she ate and you drank what she drank. Your central nervous system was in tune with her central nervous system and your metabolic system resonated closely with her metabolic system. You were also affected by how she felt about being pregnant and towards you, her unborn child.

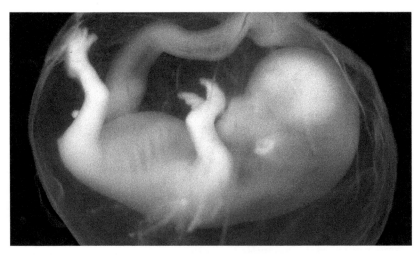

Fig 4, The in-utero baby

the brain and memory

The emotional part of the foetus's brain (the limbic brain) exists and is functioning by 12 weeks after conception ... and there is evidence that even single cells that don't have a brain can hold a memory. So it is likely that we have recorded experiences from very early on, perhaps even from our conception. The neo-cortex (our human powerhouse brain) doesn't start to develop until just before birth, so the memory that we may have of our time in our mother's womb is entirely emotional, and not recorded in our conceptual memory. This is why it is unusual for anyone to recall events prior to about two and a half years old, and we tend to think that nothing that happened before this time matters ... but it does.

early trauma ...

This early time of our life is a time of such vulnerability and sensitivity that traumatisation is extremely common. First we will look at some of the existential traumas that may happen during pregnancy and birth.

Early traumas include anything that may happen pre-birth, during birth and immediately post-birth that causes a trauma splitting reaction for the child. Some of the difficulties that may affect the child, to the extent of becoming traumatic, may occur at the following stages:

- *Conception* – if the conception is an unhappy or violent event for the mother this may affect the mother's attitude towards the child, and so affects the child
- *Pregnancy* – during the pregnancy any traumas that may happen for the mother are likely to have an impact on the child, and any medical interventions may also impact the child. Attempted abortion, if the child survives, will likely

be a major trauma for the child, and for the mother, and will continually affect how the mother feels towards her child and the development of their relationship. Does the mother really want the child or not? Does she feel scared about being pregnant and giving birth?

- *Birth* – the actual birth process may be traumatic for the child, and for the mother.
- *Post-birth* – being separated from the mother, incubated, adopted or given to others to be cared for are all likely to cause a trauma of separation. Post-birth operations such as circumcision, or other medical interventions, even if to save the child's life, are also likely to be traumatic for the child.

The conditions of the human infant in the womb and in the early stages of life are, in fact, precisely the pre-conditions of trauma: the child is helpless and utterly dependent, and so may easily feel overwhelmed. No one can reassure him intellectually of his safety and protection. He feels everything without any cognitive understanding. The only thing that makes sense to him in the beginning is his connection to his mother, because he knows her; he knows her smell, her touch, her feel, her taste, her sound and her emotional life. His connection with his father is less clear, and must come later. Even though early loving connection with the father is beneficial to the child, at this stage the mother is crucial.

birth - who decides?

Birth itself is a complex event for mother and child. Birth is possibly the most intimate event of our lives, where the quality of our relationship with our mother has a profound impact on us. The natural decision-making for the start of the birth process is likely to be an unconscious 'merged' decision between mother and child. Many hormones are released in the baby and mother to facilitate the birth process: stress hormones (adrenaline), bonding hormones (oxytocin) and rewarding hormones (dopamine) that support this extraordinary cooperation between a mother and a child in order to make a natural birth a successful event.

Both child and mother release massive amounts of the hormone oxytocin before and during birth, and in the subsequent weeks after birth. Nicknamed the 'love hormone', oxytocin is  released to ensure that the bonding between mother and child takes place. In all mammals it is what ensures that the mother cares for her young. It stimulates loving feelings. Oxytocin is also released when we do anything that makes us feel loving. When we hug another person, or feel love for him or her, this causes a release of oxytocin in us, which makes us feel good.

Several things are likely and possible during the birth process to make it a traumatic event:

- complications such as breech presentation or the umbilical cord being round the neck of the baby
- the mother may be given medication such as pain killers to help with the birth, which suppress the healthy hormonal releases, and the baby will also be medicated

- caesarean section or other medical intervention may be required (or done even though not essential), which will reduce the hormonal release, thereby diminishing the mother and child bonding ability and their pleasure of achieving a successful birth together
- the birth may stimulate the mother's unconscious memories of her own birth, which may have been a trauma for her, and so giving birth may be a retraumatising event for her

All of these will have a traumatic impact on the newborn child.

the newborn child

The basic needs of the newborn child are:

- nourishment and physical warmth
- safety and protection
- physical and emotional contact, the sense of being loved and welcomed
- being seen for who we actually are, and valued for that

The child wants nothing more than to love and be loved, to feel warm, safe, fed and welcomed; to be seen for the unique individual he is. Without any emotional contact the child may fear for his survival as much as if he is without food. The newborn child is utterly dependent on others to take care of these needs.

In order to understand this period of our life properly we have to understand just how vulnerable and helpless this unborn and newly born child is. No other animal is as vulnerable and helpless as the human child at this time of life, or for as long. Most animals can stand up soon after birth, even if in a rather wobbly way, and can negotiate their way to their mother's milk. The human child can suck, but only if given something to suck, and he can cry.

Immediately after birth is a time of rapid development of the child's brain, but since our cognitive memory comes much later, we do not have the ability to make much sense of our experiences at this stage. This means that the newborn infant cannot be reassured by words and ideas such as "it's okay, your mother will be here soon". This is meaningless for the infant, a jumble of sounds that, even though said in a soothing and loving way, make no sense to him when he is desperately missing his mother.

The child does not *know* he is safe, he only knows if he *feels* safe. And because of the familiarity with his mother, her smell, feel, sound, touch and presence, he is likely to feel safest when in contact with her, if … and it is a big 'if' … the mother actually is safe for the child to be with. In fact, whether intentionally or unintentionally, our mother was not always the safe haven she should have been, as we shall see.

Healthy bonding in action

See how the child looks for his mother? That eye-to-eye connection is as important as the milk from his mother's breast. He gains emotional nourishment, reassurance and loving connection if his mother can meet him here. He gains his first sense of himself as a separate identity from his mother by this eye contact interaction. It is his psychological and emotional anchor in a confusing new world, if it is a good connection. This brings us to the 'trauma of identity'.

who am I? – the trauma of identity

This is likely to be the earliest and most primary trauma we have experienced. It usually occurs before birth, in the very beginnings of the making of our relationship with our mother.

Does the mother see her baby as a unique individual, with his own identity, needs and wants, or does she see him as a means to gratification of her own needs and wants? Is the baby wanted for who he really is, or is he only wanted for what he can do for his mother in her delusory ideas? Does the mother, for example, unconsciously look to her child for the loving mother she didn't have, to  fulfil her own trauma needs? Was the infant's conception a happy affair, or was it violent, coercive, unloving or boring? Do the attitudes of the parents towards each other then affect how the mother feels towards the growing infant? Is the child even, perhaps, unwanted, and does his mother even consider (or attempt) abortion?

All of these things will have a significant impact on the growing child … they all leave experiential traces in the growing system of the baby … and are likely to be in us.

If we are not seen by our mother for the unique, separate individual that we are, then our connection with her has to be on her terms, a compliance with what is unconsciously required by her;

this means already, even before birth, we may have had to give up on our own wants and needs in order to survive the traumatising connection with our mother. A child cannot not have a connection with his or her mother, this is impossible … but the nature of the connection is what is key. Surviving the trauma of this connection forces the child to give up on his identity and instead he has to identify with his mother and her traumatised identity and her wants and needs.

We call this survival strategy of the trauma of identity 'identification'. I will write more about this later.

the trauma of love

As we have seen above, our first steps to developing our identity are through our relationship with our mother. If she was able to recognise our individuality and uniqueness, and she clearly wanted us, then she is able to love us clearly and unconditionally. This is a good, healthy bonding situation.

However, often this is not possible, and if the child is forced to give up on his own healthy self and identify with his mother's unconscious needs there follows a trauma of failed love. So the trauma of love is a trauma for the child of failing to gain a good loving connection with his mother.

what is love?

It helps, I think, to understand what love actually is. Love is love… as a healthy emotion it is what it is; it supports connection and bonding. But we cannot half love anything … that is not love. Love has no degrees. I either love or I don't love.

And the phenomenon of "falling in love" is not necessarily love either. It tends to be a somewhat delusional, possessive and obsessive state that rarely sees the other as they really are, and renders the person 'in love' as somewhat divorced from reality. Perhaps it is nature's way of possessing us to the matter of procreation and perpetuation of the species!

A survival form of love is conditional, compromised and delusional, and is not really love. If a mother cannot love her child without delusions, compromises or conditions she does not really love her child.

some common delusions of love:

- My mother loved me in her way
- Love heals everything
- If I love him/her enough s/he will love me
- He/she is perfect
- Money can buy love
- I can make my mother love me if I am good enough, take care of her ... etc
- One day my mother will love me ...

The primary reason for a mother to be unable to clearly feel love for her child is because she, herself, is traumatised. She is emotionally confused, and when she feels any emotion, such as love, her unresolved trauma emotions will also surface, which will prompt her to go into her survival strategies, withdrawing from emotional connection with her child. The baby then feels abandoned, alone and unloved.

Surviving a trauma of love leaves the growing child confused and not knowing clearly what love is, nor, as he grow up, how to love and how to be loved.

what do I want?

Wants and needs are different from each other. Needs are essential for our survival, as outlined above in the "basic needs of the newborn child". They are the necessities of life to ensure that we do not die: food, safety, warmth and protection, in the beginning includes the need for warm, loving emotional connection. The basic, daily physical functions such as ingestion, metabolism, excretion, breathing, and heartbeat are at the level of survival needs. When we need to eat, or excrete, we have to do so or we will die.

Wants, however, come from my will, my natural urge to exist as myself, with my identity. There is no existence without want. I am … I exist … therefore I want. If I cannot 'want' in a sense I do not exist as a real identity. Our own wants (if we can have them) are personal, individual and connected with our identity.

In any relationship trauma, whether as a child or an adult, as the victim of the trauma my 'wants' are obliterated; that is what trauma is – a situation in which what I want is overruled, not considered, not valued, trampled on and ignored.

If this happens very early in life, with the trauma of identity when we are forced to give up on our wants and instead identify with my mother's wants, then my ability to know what I want, to say what I want, to even consider that I *can* want anything in my life is distorted, even destroyed. Then we do not know what we want. Sometimes we do not even know that we *can* want. We dare not voice our wants, and we even deny them to ourselves. The trauma of identity is the splitting of the healthy 'I' from its own healthy 'wants'.

entanglement, attributions and identifications ...

entanglements

If our mother is traumatised we then become, and remain, unconsciously *entangled* with our mother's split and traumatised emotional state, to the extent that we feel her emotions and feelings as if they are our own. We are not able to distinguish between her traumatisation and ours, between her emotional life and our own. In turn she may be entangled with her mother's or father's trauma, and so we can be affected by the traumatic experiences of our grandparents and others earlier in our family.

attributions

We have to accept – and rarely question – the *attributions* our parents impose on us ... what they tell us about ourselves from a very young age ... such as:

- "You are good/bad, pretty/ugly, intelligent/stupid, too fat/too thin ..."
- "Your name will be ..." (yes, even your name may come from your parents' confusion as to who you are for them ... you may be named for a lost grandparent, an earlier, lost child etc.)
- "You are like your grandmother/grandfather/mother/father ..."

- "You have your father's temper/mother's stupidity"
- "You are a Christian/Muslim/Jew/Hindu etc ..."
- "You will grow up to be a lawyer/doctor/teacher ..."
- "You must like football/music ... follow this team ... "

These are not qualities we choose, or decide about ourselves, and may or may not be true to who we really are.

identifications

Not having a clear sense of who we are due to a trauma of identity, we then *identify* primarily with our mother and her wants. From there we will spend our life identifying with others as a way of finding some kind of identity for ourselves: our father, a sibling, a 'hero' or 'heroine', a football team, a teacher, a film star or pop siner, a lover etc. We keep looking for some certainty as to who we really are, but because we look outside of ourselves, and identify with others rather than looking at our own inner psychological state, we never find anything that really works.

consequences

as a consequence of these things we are likely to develop the following survival patterns:

- continual struggle to be loved by our mother
- continual entanglement with our mother's traumas as if they were our own
- our entangled relationship with our mother will preoccupy us to an extent all our life, even after our mother has died
- all our subsequent relationships (friends, partners, children)

become substitute 'opportunities' (through identification) to be loved by our mother and to find out who we are

- we may idealise our mother
- we may grow to hate our mother
- we may oscillate between idealisation and demonization (good mother/bad mother)
- we may copy our mother's survival strategies, relating to her as she related to her mother
- we may continually try to save our mother from her suffering, which of course we cannot do
- we will often ignore our own suffering and pain by trying to relieve our mother and everyone else of their pain
- all 'love' is a substitution since we do not know what real love is
- we may do some or all of the above with our father

Do you recognise yourself in any of this? If so then you have suffered a trauma of identity, and your sense of identity, of who you are, may be primarily through your identification with others. These are survival strategies for dealing with an early trauma of love and trauma of identity. As we continue on through this book we will learn more about these survival strategies.

the father ...

We may experience our father while we are still in the womb, hearing his voice and sensing him, which is very helpful to the child, but we do not usually really connect with our father until we are born, and even then the connection with the mother is already established and is the most important at that time for our survival. Obviously it is beneficial for the child to have a good connection with his father, but in terms of the child's sense of safety, and being able to have a good bonding, the mother is primary.

What is likely to have a greater impact on the child is the quality of the relationship between the mother and father:

- Is it a healthy loving relationship, where both parents relate most of the time from their healthy selves?
- Or is it a relationship fraught with difficulties, misunderstandings and angst?
- Do the parents live out their own unresolved traumas in their daily lives with each other, spending much of their relationship relating through their survival selves?
- Is their relationship punctuated by episodes of rage and violence or are they highly controlled and any difficulties they have are suppressed and never talked about?

On occasion if the child's connection with the mother is particularly disrupted, the child may develop a 'life-saving' connection with the father that to some extent takes the place of the one with the mother.

However this can also cause difficulties, especially if the relationship between father and child becomes too strong, perhaps too intimate, or strays too far into the sensual or even sexual. If our father has suffered a trauma of love himself he may unconsciously look to his daughter for the love he couldn't get from his mother, and this could easily lead to a confused sensual, even sexual, trauma.

sexual trauma ...

... as shown above under 'categories of traumatisation', sexual trauma is the exploitation and inappropriate sexualisation of a baby or child, incestuous sexuality, and any situation of adult enforced and inappropriate sexuality such as rape and sexual harassment that results in a trauma experience for the victim.

The last part of this sentence is important: that the person is traumatised. I remember a client telling me once that she and another little boy of the same age (about 5) had explored each other's sex organs, quite innocently ... but someone caught them and told her mother who was terribly angry. She said that her mother's anger and outrage were much more shaming and traumatising for her than the explorations with her young friend.

All human beings are sexual beings, and of course sexuality is an entirely natural part of life. Healthy sexuality is consensual, respectful and an engagement from the healthy part of ourselves with the healthy part of another person.

Sexual abuse and exploitation is sexuality that is enacted from the survival self of the perpetrator, and as such is always likely to be traumatic, since the perpetrator holds the power. I will talk a bit more about perpetrator-victim dynamics in the section on survival strategies later. Suffice to say that sexuality expressed from the survival self is primarily engaged in protecting the person from a re-stimulation of their trauma, and so is oriented towards objectifying the other person, using them in service of their own trauma survival.

So now let's move on to see what we can do about all of this ...

and so ...

... this is why trauma is such an important topic.

Just to recap:

- trauma is something we naturally avoid, and most traumas remain unaddressed and unresolved
- trauma causes the psyche to split, resulting in the emergence of a new 'self', the surviving self
- the emotions and experiences of trauma are held in our unconscious, and so it is hard for us to address them
- if our mother is not emotionally available to us as a baby, this will cause a 'trauma of identity' for us, which in turn causes a 'trauma of love'
- this affects our ability to know who we are, and to be autonomous, confident, self-authorising adults, and consequently our attempts to make healthy relationships as we grow into adulthood
- all later traumas will always, also, be a re-triggering of our original trauma
- our original trauma makes us more vulnerable to later traumatisation
- the severity of our original trauma affects our ability to manage and recover from later traumatisation

Okay, so this scenario may seem somewhat overwhelming right now. Potentially we are all influenced by past traumas, and are likely to have experienced a 'trauma of identity' and a 'trauma of love'.

I don't want to avoid this issue, because I believe that the only way we can work to resolve trauma is by facing the issue as it really is.

As human beings we have all survived thus far, for hundreds, even thousands of years. Through millennia of traumas our ancestors and family have survived; we human beings are very good at surviving, sometimes with distressing consequences of course ... but we have survived.

What we have not been so good at is resolving and healing the underlying traumas. I believe we can do this now, and from my work so far I am in no doubt about it.

We are living at a time of rapidly growing consciousness, and part of that growing consciousness includes this possibility. A hundred and fifty years ago many people believed that children were potentially evil and had to be controlled, disciplined, punished and thereby socialised; some believed that children didn't feel emotional or physical pain. Not so long ago operations were performed on children without anaesthetic, because it was believed that they didn't feel it. We are in a different time now, and I believe that our coming to terms with trauma and finding ways to resolve it are part of this growth in consciousness. Perhaps one could even say that *because* we have such pressing global dilemmas, we have to become more clear in ourselves as individuals, we have to face the impact of trauma and see if we can do something about it.

My hope is that, by understanding the processes of trauma, you can go on now to the rest of this book, and look at what you can do about it for yourself ... because no one can heal anyone else's trauma, and true autonomy is about coming to know who you really are beyond your survival strategies. There is a certain amount you can do by yourself to make a start on your journey to healing your trauma, and the next section of this book focuses on this. However, at some point you will need to find a therapist to work with ... someone who understands trauma in this way and who can help you see your survival impulses more clearly, and I will deal with that in the last section.

the task of healing

less is more!

So now let's move on to look at what healing trauma means.

Healing trauma is a step-by-step process. It cannot be rushed, and impatience will slow you down. Each person has his or her own rhythm and pace when it comes to healing, and coming to know and trust that in yourself is part of your task. This rhythm and pace is not something you can think about intellectually; it is not even fully conscious, but if you try to push yourself along with your conscious mind you will only invoke your surviving self, which will block you. You will end up fighting with yourself rather than understanding yourself. As the old adage says: you can lead a horse to water, but you can't make it drink. You can take yourself to therapy, but you cannot control your surviving self.

In this section I will suggest that you get to know the different parts of yourself, become familiar with how they work, recognise when your surviving self has been triggered, when your traumatised self is showing, and when you are comfortably in your healthy self. You will learn to recognise how the different parts of yourself relate to each other, and how  the conflicts between them are lived out in your daily life.

The task is a task of self-observation. This does *not* mean that you should do anything to change what actually happens.

It means that you are learning to understand something of *how* you work; you are increasing your self-awareness of how things are. The more self-aware you are, the more you will understand yourself, and the more you will then gain authority and clarity about yourself. You are gaining control of your life, rather than being a hostage of your life.

the overall process

First let's look at the overall process of healing trauma. This is a process of:

- **disentangling** from the traumas and feelings of others – becoming increasingly aware of what feelings you have that are truly yours, and which are confused feelings.
- **resolving** your own personal trauma of identity and trauma of love – integrating the splits within your psyche.

This is achieved by the following:

1. **becoming aware** of your survival strategies, which then helps you to . . .
2. **increase and strengthen** your healthy self, which then supports . . .
3. **integration** of your psychological splits by coming into emotional contact with your trauma

Now, you can work at the first two, and this will be helpful in your journey to healing to a considerable extent. However therapeutic help to understand your survival strategies and to help integrate the splits will be necessary in time, because I do not think we can fully let go of our survival strategies on our own.

First, in order to become aware of your survival strategies you need to understand a bit more about how the split self works.

how the split self works ...

In our daily life, when we are functioning from our healthy self, we are able to think clearly and make good decisions. However, often we are functioning from a combination of healthy/surviving/trauma parts in differing proportions.

Your ability to observe yourself will only really be possible when you are more in your healthy self than in your surviving self. The healthy self has the ability of self-reflection; the surviving self does not.

When your trauma is re-triggered, which you may find is more frequently than you realised, you will not be so good at self-observation. You must realise this. When your trauma is re-triggered you do not feel safe, and when you don't feel safe surviving that particular moment will take up all your attention. When your trauma is re-triggered your surviving self is galvanised into action, and it has only one task: to push the trauma feelings back into the unconscious, and distract you by any means available from whatever has triggered you. In that moment your surviving self takes over command from the healthy self and your ability to think clearly is gone. You are reactive in that moment, rather than responsive.

examples of different states

On page 43 are some diagrams that attempt to show how influential the different selves may be in different situations.

This first diagram (Figure 4) shows a situation in which we feel at ease. When we feel safe and comfortable the healthy self is dominant (larger), the trauma self is small and the surviving self is relatively quiet:

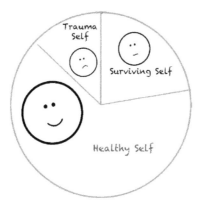

Fig. 4, Healthy self dominant

This next diagram (Fig. 5) might constitute a moment of re-triggered trauma, with the surviving self becoming very active in its attempt to keep the trauma from erupting into consciousness. In this situation, the surviving self takes charge and overrides the healthy self.

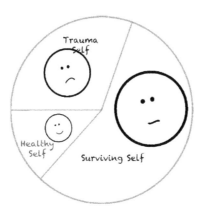

Fig. 5, Surviving self dominant

The next diagram (Fig. 6) shows a situation of major re-traumatisation, where the current survival strategies are inadequate to deal with the situation. The healthy self is very small, the trauma self is the largest, and the surviving self is not able to gain control.

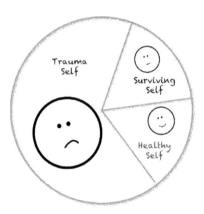

Fig. 6, Situation of major re-traumatisation: trauma self dominant, survival strategies fail

This last situation is one in which the surviving self will, as a last ditch effort to control the trauma, split again, and develop more determined strategies for maintaining control over the trauma experience. We will look at this further in the section exploring common survival strategies.

understanding structure and process

The diagrams above show structure, and indeed, after a trauma the resulting split psyche does have a more rigid and structural feel than before. The more traumatised we are, and the more vulnerable to later and further traumatisation, the more rigid becomes our psychological structure as the surviving self continues its attempts at holding the boundaries.

At the same time, even though there is a fixedness to this structure after a trauma, we are always in process. Therefore, it is rare that we would ever be fully one or other of these self parts for any length of time. Instead, we are commonly a mix, but the fluidity of our process is compromised by the structural nature of our psyche. Our experience is more fixed and less fluid, even though we may feel internally quite chaotic and helpless. The range of resources we have is limited, and feeling chaotic and helpless is part of that limited resourcefulness.

One thing that is important to understand is that we could not function from our healthy self without our survival self. The survival part allows the healthy self to function by keeping the trauma out of consciousness; if this were not to happen the healthy self would be constantly flooded and overwhelmed by the trauma feelings and experiences. For some people this is their daily life ... one of constant experiences of being overwhelmed and helpless. For these people their survival strategies barely hold on to any kind of healthy functioning.

So let's see what we can do next ...

getting to know you ...

Taking as our starting point the idea of getting to know yourself better, we will look at the characteristics and habits of the different parts of the self, starting with the healthy part of ourselves, because the healthy part of us is the one that knows, really knows, what is what. It's just that it gets confused by the other parts. So here goes ...

C'mon kiddo. Let's deal with this together.

the healthy self

When you are in your healthy self you will know it. You are able to think clearly, make good decisions, respect the truth of things, and respect yourself. You feel good about yourself. You feel effective, fulfilled and relaxed, and you can be in relationship with others and feel a range of emotions according to the current situation. Sadness, grief, anger and fear are all feelings that are appropriate in certain situations and so available to the healthy part of us. Common attributes of our healthy self include:

- having the ability for self-reflection and self-knowing
- having the ability to be ethical in our thinking and behaviour
- being interested in truth and reality
- behaviour is appropriate to the situation
- wants and needs are healthy and self-enhancing rather than self-destructive

- thinking is clear
- actions are responsive rather than reactive
- ability to be in relationship with others without losing sense of individuality
- ability to make constructive relationships
- ability to recognise and dissolve relationships that are unhealthy or destructive to oneself
- ability to be clearly available for contact and connection
- ability to remain present in intimate situations
- ability to feel a range of emotions that are a healthy response to current events
- feelings of guilt and/or shame are healthy and relate to real, current circumstances
- ability to have a good memory of the important events of the past
- ability to stay in the present

Many of us do not have these experiences often, and that is because we may be living predominantly from our surviving self. This is a sure indication that some trauma is undermining our ability to be in our healthy self.

The work of observing yourself will help you to strengthen this healthy part of yourself. Knowing when you are functioning from your healthy self is in itself helpful ... apart from anything else, you will come to recognise when you aren't.

the trauma self

The trauma self has several important characteristics:

- it is frozen in time
- it always functions at the age when the trauma happened, which may be very young
- there is likely to be a different 'trauma self' for each trauma experienced (different ages)
- in terms of the trauma of love and the trauma of identity, this 'trauma self' is very young, usually pre-verbal and even pre birth
- the trauma self is embodied emotion (with little thinking ability remaining)
- it is often wordless
- it is extremely vulnerable and helpless
- the emotional expression is cut-off and incomplete (frozen before the expression has completed)
- it is constantly looking for an opening to complete this expression/experience
- it is always looking for an opportunity to be loved, accepted and integrated

The function of the surviving self is to ignore and suppress this traumatised self, and much of our day-to-day living is caught up with this denial and suppression.

In the process of my work I have often seen that our trauma self frightens us, or disgusts us, is seen as dangerous, wilful and dark. As such we spend our whole life avoiding and denying this part of ourselves. However in my work I see that once it is really seen, it is really none of these things. It is just a lonely, unhappy and trauma-tised child longing for love and acceptance, and the opportunity to 'be'. More often than not the problem is our anticipation and fear of this moment rather than the actual moment itself. It is because of this anticipation that trauma has proved difficult to work with, and this stage of the healing – the integration of the split off parts – is best done with appropriate therapeutic support. Our innate impulse to avoid facing the trauma tends to make it very difficult, even impossible, for us to do this on our own.

how to recognise your trauma self

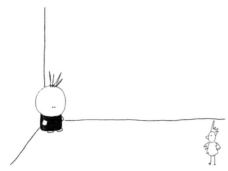

When your trauma self begins to surface several things happen, the most prominent of which is that your surviving self rushes into action. So in a sense when you see your survival self getting busy this is the most prominent indication that your trauma has been re-triggered. However there are certain experiences that belong to the trauma self and it is useful to understand and recognise these. They include:

- feeling helpless and overwhelmed
- feeling vulnerable and unsafe
- easily crying or getting aggressive
- feeling panicked
- feeling scared – if your surviving self permits that – often our fear is swamped by the survival tactics so that we don't feel it
- feeling younger than you actually are, sometimes very young
- feeling frozen and unable to act
- zoning out (dissociating)

- the strategies that you will have defined as part of your surviving self (see next section) seem very active

What you can do in this moment, if you can, include:

- allow your surviving instincts to take over – after all they have actually helped you survive in the past, and in a sense you have no choice ... this will happen anyway
- find a place of safety away from whatever has happened
- give yourself some quiet space and time to recover
- be gentle with yourself; you are in this moment close to the traumatised young child in you
- be cautious about the intentions of others – try to be with someone only if you know they are safe for you (when you are in your healthy self perhaps make a note of those people with whom you think you would feel safe when your trauma is re-triggered)
- it might be best to be on your own
- realise that your judgement is impaired and don't take any decisions or precipitous actions until you feel safer, less triggered and more in your healthy self – don't sign any documents!

If your trauma self is very strongly re-triggered you may only be able to go with the surviving self's strategies. Your helplessness may be so extreme that you cannot implement any of the other options. However, it is more usual that you are func-tioning through a mix of the selves, and there may be enough of your healthy self available to implement one or more of the above strategies to protect you.

As we shall see in the section on the surviving self, sometimes our survival strategies have paradoxically become dangerous to us, in which case when the trauma is re-triggered you may go into behaviours that to others look dangerous, such a self-harming, obsessive behaviours, disordered eating. Indeed they are likely to be dangerous if continued, and can even result in death, but for the moment they are the surviving strategies being employed by the person *because* they don't feel safe. As much as these behaviours are in the end dangerous to the self, in the critical moment they may offer the person some relief. However for anyone whose surviving mode has reached this stage I would strongly urge you to find an appropriate therapist to work with.

the surviving self

 The new self that emerges at the moment of the trauma is not our true self; its only function is to keep the trauma experience out of consciousness, and beyond that it has no faculty for self-reflection, morality, conscience or discrimination. After the trauma, the surviving self continues to develop and refine strategies that aim to fulfil this task of keeping the trauma unconscious. Since many of us have suffered a very early trauma which we may not remember, our surviving self will have developed strategies at that early time that seem to be part of who we are. Recognising these strategies is key to working with your trauma.

I think it is helpful to define three levels of surviving strategies. But please remember, these levels overlap; they are not distinct and most of you will certainly have strategies from the first two levels, and some will have strategies from all three levels. This is just a way of attempting to make sense of these strategies of survival:

first level surviving strategies:

The primary level is those immediate strategies employed at the moment of traumatisation: dissociation and splitting.

Dissociation is the process by which splitting happens. Dissociation comes and goes, whereas once the split has happened it remains. Dissociation is a process, whereas splitting is more structured and fixed.

Dissociation is always available to us after a trauma as a strategy for avoiding any re-traumatising situation. The splitting process can happen again if a later trauma is too overwhelming for our current surviving strategies, thereby causing further splits.

secondary surviving strategies:

At this level the strategies employed are 'creative' reactions to situations that re-stimulate our trauma. These become the 'habits of our personality'. They include more sophisticated means of dissociation that fall into the following categories:

- avoidance
- denial
- distraction
- suppression
- numbing
- control
- compensation
- delusionary thinking, fantasising

These basic actions become the underlying features of many of our daily activities. In fact, any activity that we do, if it has as its underlying function an avoidance of our trauma, can be operating as a survival strategy. A question to ask when thinking about an activity that you do is: does the activity that I am doing at this moment have as part of its function the avoidance of something that frightens or disturbs me?

Some examples of activities that *could* serve a surviving function are:

- working too hard, 'workaholism'
- avoiding relationships and intimate contact
- controlling oneself
- controlling others
- manipulative behaviour
- watching too much television/computer/gaming
- eating, snacking, compulsive eating, not eating
- trying to please people
- drinking alcohol
- smoking cigarettes, dope, and other social or medicinal drugs
- avoiding conflicts
- attracting conflicts
- indulging in delusionary ideas and fantasies, for example insisting that there is nothing wrong, that one's childhood was happy and stress-free
- constantly trying to please/help/save my mother (or father) and everyone else
- shopping (so-called 'retail therapy')
- drinking coffee to excess (or indeed doing anything to excess)
- sleeping – yes even sleeping or feeling tired can function as an avoidance
- and so on ....

You can fill in here any ones that you can think of that are particular to you:

- _____
- _____
- _____
- _____
- _____
- _____
- _____
- _____
- _____
- _____

Some of these activities are a normal part of life, like sleeping or eating; we have to sleep and eat, they are a natural need. It is only when they function as an avoidance of something else that they count as a survival tactic. The relevant question to ask yourself is: am I doing this as a way of avoiding something that is painful or frightening?

This does not mean that you should stop doing them, or that you should feel bad about the fact that you do them. It's information. This task is about *understanding* the processes of your life, not in order to manipulatively change them, but because understanding in itself causes change. If you really understand something, that changes it.

tertiary surviving strategies

For many of us, our surviving strategies remain in the primary and secondary phases. They will limit our lives and present us with challenges and difficulties, but they do not actively become dangerous to us.

This third level is the one at which strategies that originally came into being in order to save our life, to survive the traumatic situation, start instead to become a danger to life. In fact, we become a perpetrator and a danger to ourselves.

Survival strategies of this tertiary level would include:

- addiction to any mood/consciousness altering substances (drugs, prescribed medication, alcohol)
- serious eating disorders (bulimia, anorexia, obesity)
- active self-harming (cutting, self-denying and destructive behaviours etc)
- obsessive compulsive behaviours
- serious psychological disorders, (so-called schizophrenia, bi-polar, depression, psychosis, borderline personality disorder)
- risky and dangerous behaviour
- suicidal tendencies and fantasies
- suicide

These activities are usually the strategies of someone who comes from a traumatised family system ...

surviving the traumatised family: perpetrator-victim dynamics

If you remember the traumatised bonding system category in the section on *categories of trauma*, the surviving strategies in such a family over the generations become severe, and are predominantly based on perpetrator-victim dynamics. In other words the traumatised family system is a traumatised and continually *traumatising* family, where all interactions are perpetrator-victim interactions.

All perpetrators are victims of trauma, and their perpetration is itself a survival strategy to avoid his or her own traumatic pain by causing harm to others who are weaker. The 'stronger' take it out on the 'weaker', and the victims become perpetrators to those weaker than themselves. Thus the dynamics of this situation result in a perpetual cycle of perpetration and victimisation: victims become perpetrators, creating more victims ... and then feel victimised by the accusations of their victims. The truth of the underlying trauma can never be addressed because the shame is too great, and so the cycle continues.

In such a family system the weaker, especially children, tend to stay close to the obvious perpetrator because in this family, in a paradoxical way, that is the safest place to be. Of course it isn't really safe, but better than becoming the target. The child may then begin to behave like the perpetrator, and often 'loves' the perpetrator. Everyone in such a family has suffered both a trauma of identity and trauma of love of course, because the parents are always severely traumatised.

Any family where there is violence or sexual abuse is a traumatised family system. A child born to a mother who comes from a trau-matised family system is likely to be in great danger. This mother will have married a man who is also traumatised, because uncon-sciously she is drawn to what she knows. She may be familiar with being victimised and looks for a perpetrator to help her feel 'safe'. Her partner may come from a family that enacted incest (which would also be a traumatised family system).

In such a situation, the bonding for the child with her mother will be traumatic, due to the emotionally unavailable mother, and the child is in severe danger of being sexually abused by the father, who is likely to re-enact his own trauma. The mother, because of her trauma, is unclear in her perception of the father, her husband, and so does not 'see' the abuse potential, and unconsciously or consciously colludes with it. Even if the father does not re-enact the abuse, and manages to avoid repeating his own abusive expe-riences with his children, the child unconsciously will connect with both parents' trauma backgrounds, and copy her parents' survival strategies in order to manage her own experience. The underlying atmosphere is one of constant potential danger and unspoken fears.

a victim attitude as a survival strategy

In the actual moment of the trauma the person is a real victim, however many of us may have adopted a 'victim attitude' as a survival strategy. This is an attitude that constantly portrays one's victimhood as an excuse, rationale and explanation for the difficul-ties of one's life, and never taking responsibility for one's healing. It is itself an avoidance of the reality of one's trauma.

a perpetrator attitude as a survival strategy

The act of perpetration itself is traumatising; the causing of pain to another requires the perpetrator to avoid taking responsibility for their actions, denying and suppressing their feelings of guilt and shame, instead blaming the victim and feeling victimised themselves.

repeated and continual traumatisation in childhood

In situations of repeated traumatisation, as in an abusive childhood, the primary and secondary level surviving strategies are constantly put under pressure by repeated traumatisation. Each trauma situation causes the surviving self to produce more splits and more and more entrenched strategies to attempt to keep the trauma experiences out of consciousness. Increasingly these strategies become attempts that aim to deaden feelings, deaden the body and deaden consciousness in order not to feel the pain, despair and desperation involved.

Part of the dilemma of the seriously traumatised person is that, as their surviving self tries to deaden their feelings, this also deadens any good feelings they might have. To attempt to compensate for this and have some good and relieving feelings the person is likely to resort to drugs and alcohol, which increasingly become a source of relief as well as an avoidance of the unpleasant and frightening feelings.

the three selves

The relationship dynamics between the three self-parts is simple:

- the traumatised part yearns for recognition, expression and completion, and in this it is constantly at odds with the surviving self;
- the healthy self has similar aspirations to the traumatised self, yearning for integration, wholeness, resolution and peace, and so is also in conflict with the surviving self.
- the survival self is single-minded, it only wants to hold the splits in place.

Hence, everyone goes into therapy in an ambivalent and conflicted state. That is the nature of it. What helps is a slow increase in awareness and confidence, and making a commitment to yourself.

Here is a commitment to make to yourself:

I will take myself, my life and my trauma seriously

there is a way out!

The way out is to:

- understand these activities for what they are: activities of avoidance and denial of the pain of trauma, and profound feelings of despair, resignation and helplessness.
- recognise that if some of these are your activities this indicates that you are carrying some personal trauma.
- see this information as a 'call to arms' so to speak: find a therapist who understands this way of thinking and do the work to resolve your traumas and integrate your splits.
- do this in combination with increasing your understanding and awareness as suggested in this book.

The surviving self saved us, at one time, from the awful experience of the initial traumas. At that time we were totally inadequate and unsupported to have these experiences, and our survival literally seemed in the balance. But that isn't the case now. You are an adult now, and you can take things into your own hands.

Despite your experience of helplessness and victimisation, you are living in a different time now, and although you may *feel* helpless, you really aren't. You *can* make the decision to find help yourself; you can resolve your dilemmas and gain control and authority over your life. But only you can do this. You cannot wait for rescue or look to others to do it for you. You have to be your own rescuer; you have to take the decision and act autonomously from your healthy self in this moment; find a therapist who works with these ideas and make a commitment to yourself and your healing.

Even then, don't expect your therapist to rescue you; that is not her job. No one can heal anyone else's trauma, and the therapist can only heal hers! However, if she understands trauma from this perspective she can provide a space and a method in which you can heal yours. Moreover, you can help by starting to think about yourself within this framework, to recognise your strategies of survival, to appreciate and support your healthy self, and approach your traumatised self as it really is, a very young child, a helpless and frightened part of you. Contempt for this part of yourself is a common survival mode . . . *understanding* it can result in compassion for yourself instead.

understanding feelings ...

The main task of resolving **entanglement** is held in the question:

"how much of what I feel and experience emotionally truly belongs to me, and what have I taken on, through my attachment with my mother and father, that actually isn't me?"

Even asking this question can be enlightening. It immediately proposes the notion that not all of what I feel is actually my own, but may come from my survival need to identify with my mother, and father. How then can I decide who I am? Here is a simple questionnaire that may help with this:

- is this feeling 'my own feeling' or might it be confused with my mother's, or father's?
- is what I am feeling appropriate to what is happening in this moment?
- is the strength of feeling appropriate to what is happening, or is it more than that?
- is this a feeling that I often feel?
- is this a feeling that I often feel, but doesn't seem to have any real tangible focus?
- is this a feeling that my mother/father often seemed to feel (or avoid feeling)?

62

- are there any events that I know of in my mother/father's background to which this feeling might be appropriate?
- are there any events further back (2 to 4 generations) that I know of to which these feelings might be appropriate?

Answering these questions takes you into a different frame of thinking, one that includes the idea that your feelings may be confused with those unexpressed trauma feelings of others.

You may feel that you can't answer all of the questions. Regard them as potentially stimulating to your less conscious sense of yourself and see what answers might pop into your head.

Even though your answer to the question: are my feelings appropriate to the current circumstances? may be "no", that doesn't mean that you don't have such feelings. Since we split off our own trauma feelings in order to survive, the feelings connected with *your* trauma are indeed yours. In addition, since the traumas of identity and of love are essentially pre-verbal and pre-cognitive memory, it is the case that you genuinely may not know the answer to the question. However, it *is* possible that asking these questions prompts answers that may feel right to you. And since this book is not about healing the splits, but only about stimulating your understanding and insight, such understandings I hope will prompt you to find the right help.

feelings and trauma

Understanding our feelings means realising that some feelings can function as survival strategies; some feelings keep us away from other feelings. I call these 'instead of' feelings, since they function as substitutes for feeling the deeper, more painful feelings.

For example, I know from my own history and experience that for a long time it would take very little to reduce me to helpless, sniffly crying. I couldn't help myself, and sometimes it would last for hours. I never felt any resolution, and the experience was ultimately unsatisfying and out of my control, and it was often very difficult to understand why I felt as I did. I was left feeling vulnerable, a bit silly, confused and ashamed. I now understand that crying in this way actually protected me from stronger, clearer feelings that I instinctively feared.

This is considered a common experience for many women, whereas a more common experience for men may be that they suddenly, and seemingly unaccountably, become aggressive, angry and 'lose it'. (This of course is a gross generalisation, and some women may resort to aggression and some men may resort to endless morose tears, or feeling depressed.)

A good question to ask yourself in such a situation is:

"What might these feelings be helping me avoid?"

Here's some information I have discovered about feelings and trauma. Our emotional expression falls into two distinct categories: healthy feelings and survival feelings.

qualities of healthy feelings:

- are appropriate to the current situation
- have a beginning, a climax and an ending
- endure for minutes only
- leave one feeling finished, better and ready to move on to the next thing
- involve the whole self, body and mind

- the expressed emotion is clearly one emotion (e.g. grief, rage, terror, fear, love, joy)

This would also include the appropriate expression of trauma feelings in a current deliberate therapeutic healing environment.

whereas the qualities of survival feelings are:

- not appropriate to the current situation
- seem to rise and fall, but never peak and do not have a clear ending
- often last for a long time without resolution
- leave one feeling exhausted, frustrated and confused
- often are accompanied by an experience of a lump in the throat or tightness and congestion in the chest and body, or other 'blocked' experiences
- the expression is often confused and it is difficult to name the feeling clearly

Again, my suggestion at this stage is that you absorb this information, see if it makes sense to you and don't give yourself a hard time about it. If this applies to you just ask yourself the question above, and mark it down as potential evidence of trauma, and as one of your survival strategies.

shame and guilt ...

Shame and guilt in their healthy forms have a morally moderating and protective function. If you have done something that contravenes your own healthy self's sense of ethics you may feel ashamed, and if your actions have caused pain or harm to another you may feel guilt.

However shame and guilt are often used as weapons of perpetration and control, and your present experiences and feelings may be continually pervaded by feelings of unaccountable shame and guilt. They usually come together since when used in this way, the perpetrator shames the child and accuses them of doing something that harms the perpetrator, so that the child feels guilty.

So in your quest to understand your surviving strategies, if you are frequently beset by feelings of shame and guilt that do not have a clear current rational cause, then these too are likely to be defences against feeling the deeper trauma feelings, for  example rage and terror. However, don't forget, they may also be feelings that you are entangled with; the shame and guilt you feel may relate to and be confused with the shame and guilt of your mother or father. Traumatised families dealing in perpetrator-victim dynamics always harbour strong feelings of guilt and shame, and use them as a means of control and perpetration.

trust ...

Trauma seriously impairs, even destroys, our trusting ability. In the relational trauma situation we are helpless and vulnerable to the will and power of another. This affects our trust in that person, and can impair, and even destroy, our trust in ourselves and in life.

trusting you

One of the main reasons for becoming aware of your surviving strategies is connected with the issue of trust. The splitting that happens during the trauma of identity is an experience of the loss of self, and as such is in a sense a betrayal of the self: one part of the self is forced to abandon another. The surviving self forces the healthy self to abandon the traumatised self. We can't control this as we have seen; it is the instinctive and natural reaction to the overwhelming trauma situation. Nevertheless, it leaves us in a state of mistrust and confusion within ourselves.

The opposing and different natures of our healthy self and our surviving self cause us much confusion and mistrust of ourselves, because we do not know who we really are.

If you are to trust yourself you need to have an idea of which self you can trust, and recognising which self is active in any moment will help you to do this. Put simply, you can trust your healthy aspirations and, as frightening as it may seem, you can also trust the traumatised part of you. The one that presents more difficulties is, of course, the surviving self. However, you *can* trust this surviving self to do its job! The surviving self parades itself as 'the truth' and as being trustworthy … that is part of its style, but it actually trades in illusions, lies and distortions of the truth with the sole intention of keeping the trauma out of awareness.

Children must and do trust their caregivers. They have no option; an infant's survival depends on his parents. Children arrive in the world full of love … and they love their parents, even if a parent frightens them, because the child doesn't know how else to be with his parents. He may at times hate them, but this will cause him shame and guilt, adding to his confusion. When the parent fails the child's trust, the child is lost, without safety and protection, adrift and helpless. Yet the child must continue to trust his parents. The child then becomes confused as to what trust is: who is really trustworthy? Who can he trust? And over time his ability to trust his own idea of who is trustworthy becomes distorted; his trust in his own judgement fails and he falls prey to trusting the untrustworthy.

Because we have to trust others to an extent to get through life, an adult whose internal ability to assess trustworthiness is damaged will repeatedly trust people she probably shouldn't, in situations that may not be safe for her. She may repeatedly take dubious risks and consequently suffer repeated traumatisation throughout her life. So, people who suffered more severe early traumatisation are likely to suffer more traumas later in life than those who have not experienced such severe trauma.

trusting others ...

Here is an interesting thought:

no one is 100% trustworthy 100% of the time

Most of us will at times go into our survival self, and in that state our trustworthiness and reliability diminishes dramatically.

Here's another thought:

trust is never fixed ... it changes, depending on the circumstances

If we include the early traumas of identity and love in our thinking about our relation-ships with others, we can conclude that most people (perhaps all) are likely to have suffered some kind of trauma at some time in their life. This means that at times others may not always act in the way we expect or wish.

It is helpful to understand that when people you are close to act in ways that seem to frustrate your efforts, irritate you, keep you at a distance, or don't seem to make sense, it is possible that they are functioning from their surviving self. This means that something has triggered their own trauma – perhaps even something you have done or said – and their surviving self has sprung into action.

This applies to your mother and father, siblings and other relations, partners and friends, work colleagues, and anyone you come across during your day. If your mother or father is functioning from his or her surviving self, that is not their healthy self. As you become familiar with your own surviving self and its strategies, you will also become better at understanding others' behaviour, which will help you find better ways of relating, or deciding when to leave destructive relationships. However, do remember, if someone else is functioning from their survival self, something has re-triggered their trauma, perhaps something you have done or said . . . it is not something the person can control, it is their natural reaction to the surfacing of difficult and frightening feelings.

healthy relationships

Healthy relationships are those that function primarily from the healthy selves of both people, and the best way that this can happen is through the process of resolving our personal traumas so that we spend more of our life functioning from our healthy self.

Here is a diagram showing the different kinds of relationship that may be taking place between two people:

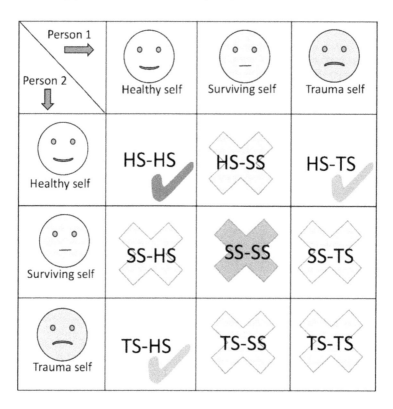

Fig. 7, who is relating to whom? (original diagram by Franz Ruppert)

Obviously, the easiest and most productive configuration is if both people are functioning from their healthy selves (HS-HS) since both are able to see each other clearly, remain in the present and emotions are appropriate to the current situation.

Slightly less easy but also potentially productive is if one person is functioning from their more traumatised self and the other from their healthy self, because at least the person in their healthy self will be able to see the other clearly and relate to their vulnerability (HS-TS and TS-HS).

In the SS-TS situation, one person functions from their trauma self and the other in survival mode: the person in their surviving mode will not see the traumatised self clearly since their own trauma is also likely to be present (otherwise they wouldn't be functioning from survival mode). Communication is likely to miss the mark, and be unhelpful to the person who is struggling with their trauma feelings.

The most difficult and entangling configuration, and the one where any good outcome is impossible, is if both people are relating from their surviving selves (SS-SS). Neither has the clarity to see or hear the other since both feel threatened and are preoccupied with keeping their trauma out of consciousness. The communication is likely to be frustrating, endlessly repetitive and with little possibility of finding a resolution. Such situations are deeply entangled and it is impossible for either to find a solution; both become perpetrator and victim as their individual traumas are replayed in some form. The best option is for both to go and find some private safe space to recover and gain more access to their healthy self. Many couples frequently get into this kind of frustrating engagement.

healthy relationships

Here are some characteristics of healthy relationships for you to think about:

- the relationship is one of equals
- difference is allowed
- there are common interests, goals and values
- there is an openness to the continual development of the other
- expectations of the other are realistic
- both partners recognise and are willing to deal with their own traumas
- reality is valued over illusions
- if necessary separation with mutual agreement, respect and care is possible

and here are some characteristics of unhealthy relationships:

- possessive and clinging behaviour
- each pushing for the other to change
- high expectations of the other
- idealisation of and/or disapproval of the other
- inability to understand the other and to feel understood
- characterised by dominance and submission
- lack of common interests and goals
- dominated by illusions of love such as: 'love conquers all', 'all parents love their children', 'If I love this person enough he/she will love me', 'I can buy love with money and gifts'
- characterised by illusions of forgiveness and reconciliation

This last one is often the way that people find to 'resolve' their relational difficulties, but because they deny and diminish the underlying issue, the 'forgiving' and 'reconciliation' are temporary,

73

unreal and have more to do with survival than reality and a real resolution.

Remember, as easy as it is for your trauma to be re-triggered, projecting you into survival mode, it is just as easy for everyone else. We are all vulnerable to it. If we can recognise this in each other, things will go better, we will understand each other better, be able to stay away from entangled and unproductive communication, and feel more compassion for each other. Two people communicating from their survival selves are two people whose trauma is very close, and so underneath they are frightened and vulnerable.

so now what?

In this book so far we have covered some of the processes that contribute towards resolving trauma:

- we have looked in detail at what trauma is and how it works, the split structure that occurs after trauma and the emergence of the surviving self as the guardian of the boundaries of the splits
- we have looked at how you can improve your relationships with others by understanding survival processes in yourself and them
- and we have looked at ways in which you can become aware of your survival strategies, getting to know your different selves, thereby strengthening your healthy self

These are invaluable steps towards resolving trauma. But resolving trauma means, in the end, integrating the split parts within you. My belief at this time is that this is not something you can do on your own, as I have said before, so I will now discuss briefly the form of therapy that I know works.

identity therapy ...

At this point you may be thinking about finding a therapist in order to take the next step: integrating the splits in your psyche, addressing the question "who am I?". We can do a lot for ourselves by increasing our understanding of the dynamics involved, explaining some of our behaviours and attitudes, and becoming aware of our surviving strategies. This does increase our sense of control and self-authority, but it doesn't allow for actual integration of the splits. The power of our surviving self as the interrupter of such work continually creates internal conflicts.

finding a therapist ...

Finding a therapist who is familiar with the ideas presented here is important and, at this stage, not easy since this perspective and work is fairly new. However this will change over the next few years, as the work becomes better known.

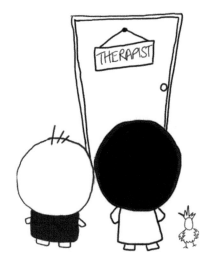

I'm going to talk here about the therapy as I do it. Other therapists may vary in their approach, but provided they have a good grounding in the ideas presented here, and they use the Intention Method, using the 'sentence of intention', I am sure they will be helpful to you.

the intention method ...

The Intention Method was developed over many years by Professor Ruppert, and is a way in which we can explore the less conscious aspects of our psyche with extraordinary accuracy, thereby gaining insight and understanding of how we have been impacted by trauma. We are provided with a perception of our issues that reaches underneath our usual perception of ourselves, often showing the root causes of our difficulties quickly, effectively and truthfully. Over time it can also provide a means of encountering our trauma, when we are ready, in a safe and well-regulated way, allowing us to remain in charge of the work throughout the process.

The method is based on a concept of *resonance*. What we mean by this is the ability of two or more beings to come into mutual resonance with each other, and share information, emotional data and experiences. This is similar to the bonding process between a mother and her child, and happens through what has been called 'limbic brain resonance', where the emotional (limbic) part of the brain of one being comes into a resonance with the limbic brain of another. It's a bit like 'home sharing' in computer language. The 'intention method' uses this phenomenon to explore the stores of our memory that we don't consciously recall.

The 'sentence of intention'

The sentence of intention is the starting point, and provides the framework for this exploration. First, you establish what your intention is at this time for this particular exploration session.

Your 'sentence of intention' might be something like: "I want to feel more confident", or "I want to understand why I don't get on with my sister" or "How have I been affected by the unspoken trauma in my family?". What you want to explore and how this is stated is entirely up to you. It may take you a little time to gain clarity about what you want from the session, and the therapist will wait patiently until you have done so, but the exploration cannot start until you have defined what your intention is.

When you are ready you will write your 'sentence of intention' up on a flipchart board, and it then forms the framework for the exploration you will do. Once this is done your exploration can begin.

yes, but what happens?

Each word in your intention will have its own particular meaning in your unconscious, and so can provide you with information that addresses the issue in some way. In a group you would choose group members to resonate with each of the words from your sentence, and they simply follow whatever their resonant experience is. Sometimes the information that surfaces seems to have a direct relation to the meaning of a particular word, and sometimes it doesn't. As the work progresses information and experiences arise in you and in the resonators that provides increasing insight and shifts in perception about your issue. These insights might include . . .

- seeing the confusion of the traumatised system (the family) sometimes over several generations;
- understanding the impact of this on your parents' ability to care for you;
- increasing your awareness of your survival strategies;
- strengthening your connection with your healthy 'I';
- helping you to acknowledge your own trauma;

- helping you to distinguish your own feelings from those of others;
- helping you to distinguish truth from illusions;
- helping you to separate from entangled relationships;
- learning to keep your own boundaries;
- experiencing yourself as traumatised in a contained, managed and safe way;
- integrating the trauma by coming into contact with that part;
- living more and more in healthy, constructive relationships.

Remember... you are in charge of your healing ...

Through the Intention Method you can explore your inner world, your psyche, and come to understand more fully what your life's experiences have been, who you really are. A definition of identity is all of the accumulated experiences that you have had since your conception, including the good times and the bad, including your happy experiences and your trauma. To deny any of it diminishes who you are, your identity. And since trauma survival results in experiences being split off and then denied, it is up to you to reclaim yourself.

You can of course ask your parents and family about your early life, but you have to remember that people, including your parents, are liable to miss out the tough stuff! After all our parents are also likely to function from their survival self, and they too would rather not speak about things that cause them pain. So what they tell us may be true of course, but it may be only partially true … and it may not be true at all. So you have to take responsibility to find out for yourself, and remember …

... everything that you have ever experienced is within you, and you can access this information ... when you are ready to take the risk ...

taking yourself seriously

IIntegrating the psychological splits that are the result of trauma means making this a priority in our lives ... taking yourself and your trauma seriously and putting yourself first. We all have a responsibility to put ourselves first and, step by step, to come into better, more loving contact with ourselves.

Loving yourself enough to put yourself first is not selfish, it isn't narcissistic self-absorption and self-obsession – these are the surviving modes of the person who cannot love themselves because of their trauma with a mother who couldn't love them either. They keep trying to find love in distorted surviving ways.

Loving yourself is self-valuing; it is innate, natural, wholesome and healthy. You cannot really love another if you do not love yourself. In order to be able to be in a good relationship with another you must be in a good and loving relationship with yourself. In order to respect another person you must first respect yourself. In order to trust others you first must trust yourself.

Integration means being able to put yourself first in a clear and honest way. It means understanding that you cannot help or heal your traumatised mother or father, and that you never could. No one can heal anyone else's trauma ... you can only heal your own. It means recognising if I was not wanted, not love and not protected.

From here you have the clarity of vision and thought to know what is the right action in a given situation; you know what help you can give another, and what you can't; you have realistic ideas of what is possible in your world and a good sense of how to go forward.

So the hope that is available is this: you are responsible, you do have autonomous ability in your healthy self, and if you can get clearer as to your healthy intentions, then you will know how to go forward, how to take the next step …

a word about the world ...

Understanding the reality of trauma means understanding that we live in a highly traumatised world that is continually re-traumatising its people. Political aggression, terrorism, conflict, war, corporate and economic dominance perpetuate this situation as the perpetrator-victim cycle continues. We are controlled and ruled by the traumatised who act from their own survival instincts. This is a frightening perception, and one that provokes a sense of helplessness and overwhelm in us. To think of this situation immediately puts us more in touch with our own personal trauma and prompts us to look away. It seems like an insuperable problem.

but ...

If we each take full responsibility for healing our own trauma we then make better decisions for ourselves, and can exercise the power that we do have to share our understanding with others. I do not know what this means in the end, but the impact of a growing number of people whose perception is increasingly cleared of the confusions of trauma will have an effect. It can influence, for example, how we vote when we have the opportunity, who we vote for, who we work with and how we relate to our work colleagues, our profession and our politicians and journalists, who we choose to follow, to recommend and to avoid.

Above all it affects how we are able to relate to our children and help them to develop into healthy adults. Your children may already have suffered a trauma of love with you, but as you work with your own trauma and become clearer in your psyche, the clearer and more real and honest will be the environment you create while your children grow and develop. Children know how their parents are … and they know when their parents are healthy in their psyche, and when they are not.

about me ...

I have been a psychotherapist in private practice since 1989. I met Professor Franz Ruppert in 2004 and have been studying with him ever since. From 2010 my work has developed entirely along the model Franz Ruppert proposes.

When I began to work according to these ideas and practice it completely changed my approach to psychotherapy. I understood that unresolved trauma, particularly early attachment trauma and the entanglement with earlier traumas in the family, underlies all of our psychological difficulties. I find the Intention Method an elegant process that combines intelligence and integrity, safety and effectiveness. The ethics of working with trauma – the stance of the therapist, the attention to detail, and the need for the authority of the work to remain firmly with the client – present a clarity and discipline for the therapist that I value and enjoy.

www.vivianbroughton.com
info@vivianbroughton.com

about karen

Karen McMillan travels the world working as a holistic therapist, cartoonist and illustrator. Karen is thrilled to be collaborating with Vivian on this project and is passionate about the understanding and healing of oneself that Vivian's work brings to individuals.

www.karenveramcmillan.com
www.aworkinprogress.co.uk

further reading

Franz Ruppert:

Trauma, Bonding and Family Constellations: Understanding and healing injuries of the soul.

Splits in the Soul: Integrating traumatic experiences

Symbiosis and Autonomy: Symbiotic trauma and love beyond entanglements

Trauma, Love and Fear: How the Constellation of the Intention supports Healthy Autonomy

Early Trauma: Pregnancy, Birth and First Years of Life

Vivian Broughton:

The Heart of Things: Understanding Trauma – Working with Constellations

All published by Green Balloon Publishing,
www.greenballoonbooks.co.uk

Milton Keynes UK
Ingram Content Group UK Ltd.
UKHW011910090224
437550UK00013B/391